# YOU KNOW YOU'RE A GOLF ADDICT WHEN...

Written and Illustrated by
**Jerry King**

**Crest Publishing House**
(A JAICO ENTERPRISE)
G-2, 16 Ansari Road, Darya Ganj
New Delhi-110 002

© 2001 Boston America Corp.

All rights reserved. No part of this book may be reproduced or transmitted in any form or by any means, electronic or mechanical including photocopying, recording or by any information storage and retrieval system, without permission in writing from the publishers.

ISBN 81-242-0239-7

First Indian Edition: 2001

*Published by:*
Pentagon Press, New Delhi
in arrangement with
BOSTON AMERICA CORP.
125 Walnut Street, Watertown, MA 02172
*Exclusively for:*
CREST PUBLISHING HOUSE
New Delhi

*Printed by:*
Elegant Printers
New Delhi-110064

Authorised reprint edition for sale in India, Nepal, Pakistan, Bangladesh, Sri Lanka, Malaysia & Indonesia

"I think the great thing
about the game of golf is
you never master it,
no matter what level you play.
Even Jack Nicolas, Arnold Palmer
--the greatest players in the game--
have never mastered it
and nobody will."

-Vince Gill
Country Star

# YOU KNOW YOU'RE A GOLF ADDICT WHEN...

**You actually think your golf attire is attractive.**

# YOU KNOW YOU'RE A
# GOLF ADDICT
## WHEN...

**Your game is 4 parts social: one part golf.**

# YOU KNOW YOU'RE A GOLF ADDICT WHEN...

**Your golf game puts your personal relationships in jeopardy.**

# YOU KNOW YOU'RE A GOLF ADDICT WHEN...

**You get lots of golf gifts and actually think they look attractive.**

# YOU KNOW YOU'RE A
# GOLF ADDICT
### WHEN...

**You take a second job to support your golf habit.**

# YOU KNOW YOU'RE A GOLF ADDICT WHEN...

**Including a little wager makes your game more fun.**

# YOU KNOW YOU'RE A GOLF ADDICT WHEN...

**Some things at your place are sparkling clean.**

# YOU KNOW YOU'RE A GOLF ADDICT WHEN...

**You're very serious about your golf analysis.**

# YOU KNOW YOU'RE A
# GOLF ADDICT
### WHEN...

**You're always ready for a game.**

# YOU KNOW YOU'RE A GOLF ADDICT WHEN...

**Your competitive spirit prevails in all forms of golf.**

# YOU KNOW YOU'RE A GOLF ADDICT WHEN...

**Minor aches and pains don't effect your desire to play.**

# YOU KNOW YOU'RE A
# GOLF ADDICT
## WHEN...

**You play golf to relieve stress.**

# YOU KNOW YOU'RE A
# GOLF ADDICT
### WHEN...

## You find televised golf exciting.

*"Golf is the study of a lifetime and you can find a new secret at least every seven days, if you look for it."*
--Judy Bell, President, United States Golf Association

# YOU KNOW YOU'RE A
# GOLF ADDICT
### WHEN...

**A bad golf shot is never your fault.**

# YOU KNOW YOU'RE A
# GOLF ADDICT
## WHEN...

**You'd sell your soul for "The Perfect Swing".**

# YOU KNOW YOU'RE A GOLF ADDICT WHEN...

**You feel compelled to explain, in detail, everyone of your shots.**

# YOU KNOW YOU'RE A
# GOLF ADDICT
### WHEN...

**Once each golf season you do your lawn whether it needs it or not.**

# YOU KNOW YOU'RE A
# GOLF ADDICT
### WHEN...

**You think everyone in the world is a golf enthusiast.**

# YOU KNOW YOU'RE A
# GOLF ADDICT
## WHEN...

**You have trouble maintaining your friendships.**

# YOU KNOW YOU'RE A GOLF ADDICT WHEN...

**Your vacations always consist of low rate golf packages.**

# YOU KNOW YOU'RE A GOLF ADDICT WHEN...

**Your house slowly turns into a storage place for golf equipment.**

# YOU KNOW YOU'RE A
# GOLF ADDICT
## WHEN...

**The only way you can communicate is by using golf reference.**

# YOU KNOW YOU'RE A
# GOLF ADDICT
### WHEN...

**The pros request your removal from the course.**

# YOU KNOW YOU'RE A GOLF ADDICT WHEN...

**You're always ready to subscribe to a new golf magazine.**

# YOU KNOW YOU'RE A GOLF ADDICT WHEN...

**You never miss an opportunity to practice.**

# YOU KNOW YOU'RE A GOLF ADDICT WHEN...

**You own every type of golf club ever made.**

# YOU KNOW YOU'RE A
# GOLF ADDICT
## WHEN...

**You take golf so seriously that it effects your personal life.**

# YOU KNOW YOU'RE A GOLF ADDICT WHEN...

**Your golf season lasts all year long.**

# YOU KNOW YOU'RE A GOLF ADDICT WHEN...

**You're forced to limit the amount of equipment you carry.**

# YOU KNOW YOU'RE A GOLF ADDICT WHEN...

"IT'S MY GREAT GRANDMA'S BIRTHDAY. WHAT BETTER WAY TO CELEBRATE IT THAN A GOOD ROUND OF GOLF?"

**Every occasion is to golf.**

# YOU KNOW YOU'RE A GOLF ADDICT WHEN...

**If golfing all day isn't enough, you spend the remaining evenings in the clubhouse rehashing your game.**

# YOU KNOW YOU'RE A
# GOLF ADDICT
## WHEN...

## You play so often that you have each course memorized.

*"Golf is much more an art form than it is a science."*
*--Judy Bell, President, United States Golf Association*

# YOU KNOW YOU'RE A GOLF ADDICT WHEN...

**You have no friends on the course.**

# YOU KNOW YOU'RE A
# GOLF ADDICT
## WHEN...

**Aside from regular golf, you play night golf, snow golf, miniature golf and video golf**

# YOU KNOW YOU'RE A GOLF ADDICT WHEN...

**Your golf clubs give a hint to how your game went.**

# YOU KNOW YOU'RE A GOLF ADDICT WHEN...

**Within a matter of minutes you're able to both love and hate the game of golf.**

# YOU KNOW YOU'RE A GOLF ADDICT WHEN...

**Everyone in front of you plays too slow and everyone behind you plays too fast.**

# YOU KNOW YOU'RE A
# GOLF ADDICT
## WHEN...

**Your golf game takes precedence over most responsibilities.**

# YOU KNOW YOU'RE A GOLF ADDICT WHEN...

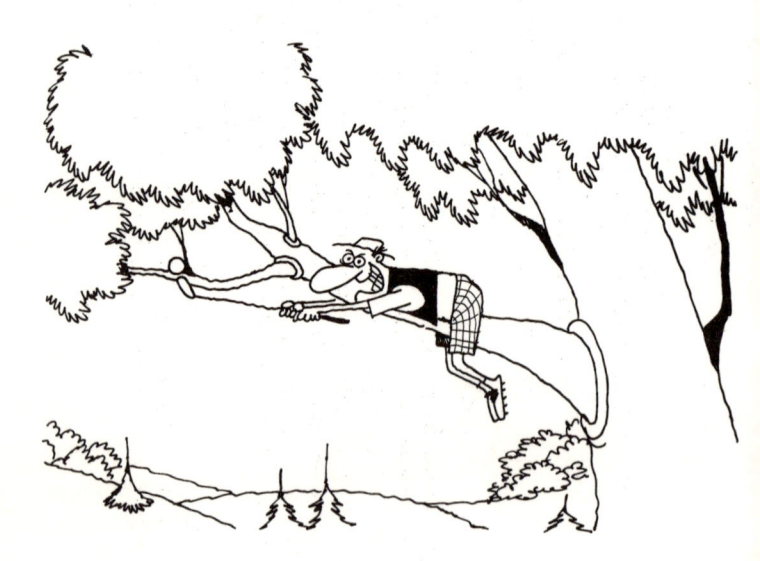

**No lie is unplayable.**

# YOU KNOW YOU'RE A
# GOLF ADDICT
## WHEN...

**85% of the words you use on the course are swear words.**

# YOU KNOW YOU'RE A
# GOLF ADDICT
## WHEN...

**Golf takes priority over sex.**

# YOU KNOW YOU'RE A
# GOLF ADDICT
### WHEN...

**You're on the mailing list of every golf store in your state.**

# YOU KNOW YOU'RE A
# GOLF ADDICT
## WHEN...

**You play strictly by the rules no matter how casual the game.**

# YOU KNOW YOU'RE A GOLF ADDICT WHEN...

**You never, ever play for just fun.**

# YOU KNOW YOU'RE A GOLF ADDICT WHEN...

**Postponing or canceling a golf game is never a consideration.**

# YOU KNOW YOU'RE A GOLF ADDICT WHEN...

**You belong to every golf league in town.**

# YOU KNOW YOU'RE A
# GOLF ADDICT
## WHEN...

*If they would water these fairways maybe I could have a good shot!*

**A bad golf shot is never your fault.**

# YOU KNOW YOU'RE A GOLF ADDICT WHEN...

**You invest in every golf gimmick that promises to make you better.**

# YOU KNOW YOU'RE A GOLF ADDICT WHEN...

**You hold up everyone behind you to look for free balls.**

# YOU KNOW YOU'RE A GOLF ADDICT WHEN...

You imitate the pro's actions even though you have no idea what you're doing.

# YOU KNOW YOU'RE A
# GOLF ADDICT
## WHEN...

**'72 holes just isn't enough.**

# YOU KNOW YOU'RE A
# GOLF ADDICT
## WHEN...

**You give unqualified advice to the other golfers.**

# YOU KNOW YOU'RE A GOLF ADDICT WHEN...

## You get a special thrill from a free ball.

*"Golf is like a butterfly, just when you think you've caught it, it flies away."*
--Judy Bell, President, United States Golf Association